GUNFIGHTERS

Volume 14

Tales of the Wild West Series

Rick Steber

Illustrations by Don Gray

NOTE
GUNFIGHTERS is the fourteenth book in
the Tales of the Wild West Series

GUNFIGHTERS
Volume 14
Tales of the Wild West Series

Bonanza Publishing
Box 204
Prineville, Oregon 97754

INTRODUCTION

The names of the gunfighters are legendary: Butch Cassidy and the Sundance Kid, Doc Holliday, Jesse James, Billy the Kid, Pat Garrett, Henry Plummer, Bat Masterson, Wyatt Earp, Wild Bill Hickok.... These men, and others like them, epitomize the image of the Wild West.

The gunfighting era was born in the late 1830s when Samuel Colt patented his single-barreled pistol with a revolving bullet chamber. But the gunfighter was not common on the frontier until after the Civil War when renegade bands of Confederate soldiers refused to surrender. Their lawless ways spread as they stole from the hated Union bankers and the monopolistic railroads, rustled from wealthy ranchers and killed anyone who dared stand in their way.

Railhead towns, where the great Texas cattle drives ended, generated more than their fair share of gunfights. In these towns the distinction between the law and the outlaw was a fine line and many times the men who wore badges worked both sides of the fence.

It generally fell to the individual to uphold the law and nearly every western man strapped a six-shooter to his hip. If a man's cattle or horses were stolen, if his home was ransacked or his family attacked, it was up to that man to track down the guilty party and administer swift justice.

Around the turn of the 19th century the free-roaming gunfighters found the wild country could no longer hide them as technology, in the form of telegraphs and telephones, cut off escape routes. Even though the era of the gunfighter had drawn to a close, writers and movie makers, using the colorful backdrop of the Old West, turned the frontier gunfighters into larger-than-life folk heros, folk heros who will never die.

LIFE OF CRIME

A couple weeks before Christmas 1896 a local man came into the sheriff's office in Blackwell, Kansas with exciting news.

"There's two men out at the old Benjamin place and they're plannin' on holdin' up the bank. I overheard 'em talkin'. An' one of the men is missin' three fingers."

That got the sheriff's attention because "Dynamite Dick" Clifton, a notorious bank and train robber, had lost three fingers on his left hand. The sheriff wanted to know, "Which hand?"

"Left," said the local and he followed it up with, "I'll get the reward, won't I?"

"You might have to split it," the sheriff told him. He jumped to his feet, threw open the door and called into the street, "I'm organizing a posse to bring in Dynamite Dick Clifton. If you're the one that get's him, you'll be entitled to half the $3,500 reward. Any takers?"

Six men quickly volunteered and the sheriff led them out of town toward the Benjamin ranch where they found two horses, saddled and ready to ride, hitched to a post in front of the house. The sheriff directed the men to surround the house and when they were in place he hollered, "We know you're in there! Come out with your hands up!"

At the sound of his voice two men rushed through the open door, firing as they came. Three members of the posse turned tail and ran but the other three and the sheriff stood their ground and returned fire, wounding one of the men and killing the other.

The dead man was not Dynamite Dick, but a petty criminal named Buck McGregg. The wounded man turned out to be the real catch when he was identified as Ben Cravens, a cattle rustler and killer. He was jailed temporarily but escaped and returned to his life of crime.

BUTCH & SUNDANCE

There was no way to foresee from his strict religious upbringing -- his father had come to Utah with the original Mormon handcart brigade -- that Robert Parker would turn to lawless ways.

But Parker was befriended by a small time criminal named Mike Cassidy and at age 16 the boy left home to ride the outlaw trail using the alias George Cassidy. He traveled to Colorado robbing trains and holding up banks and, for a time, worked in a butcher shop. Thereafter he became known as Butch Cassidy.

Butch was arrested for cattle rustling in 1892 and sentenced to a two-year stretch in the Wyoming State Penitentiary. After his release he formed the notorious Wild Bunch to rob trains and banks.

By the turn of the century the law was closing in. Butch and one of his outlaw friends, Harry Longabaugh - better known as the Sundance Kid, and Etta Place, Sundance's girlfriend, fled to South America. For a while the trio operated a cattle ranch in Argentina. Early in 1908 Butch and Sundance were in a gunfight with Bolivian soldiers and Sundance was killed.

Butch returned to the United States and lived under the name William Phillips. In 1910 he moved to Spokane, Washington and established Phillip's Manufacturing Company which produced business equipment. After losing the company during the depression he made several unsuccessful trips to his old haunts, searching for loot he had buried while riding with the Wild Bunch.

His last days were spent trying to market a manuscript he had written, titled *The Bandit Invincible,* based on his life as Butch Cassidy. He found no takers and died in 1937 at Broadacres, the Spokane County poor farm.

THE MAIL RUN

"Trying to run a stage line was nothing but a headache. Something new every day. One time it might be a big storm washed out the road, or blowdowns blocking the road, a broken spring, a wheel gone bad, a runaway, lost mail, a driver who failed to show up for his run. You name it - it happened. We even had a few holdups," related Charles Barnard, who held the contract at the turn of the century to deliver mail from the Willamette Valley to towns along the northern Oregon coast.

"I remember one of my stagecoach drivers was held up at gunpoint, relieved of the mail and ordered to drive away. By the time he reached the express station he had worked himself into quite an agitated state of mind. He claimed that from then on he would pack a gun and bragged that if anyone tried to hold him up again he would plug them.

"I told him to leave his gun at home. Carrying a gun was a bad idea. He would be apt to get himself killed.

"The driver ignored me. Several weeks later he was stopped once again and this time the road agent had the nerve to say, 'Remember me? I'm the fellow that held you up a few weeks back.'

"The driver nodded his head and in a shaky voice asked, 'Why me? Why are you picking on me?'

"The robber laughed. 'Guess you're just unlucky.' Then, according to one of the passengers, the road agent noticed the driver's holstered revolver and went on to say, 'Better give me that six-gun. As nervous as you are, that thing might happen to go off and hurt someone. We don't want that to happen, do we?'

"Apparently the driver took the warning to heart. Never again did he wear a sidearm, and as luck would have it, he was never robbed again, either."

BILLY THE KID

He was born Henry McCarty, took the name William Bonney but became known far and wide as "Billy the Kid".

Some who knew Billy described him as a nice boy, bucktoothed with a winsome smile. They claimed he was polite and a talented musician. But they also warned of his fiery temper that could erupt with little provocation.

Billy the Kid was 17 when he killed his first man, in a quarrel with a burly blacksmith who threw Billy to the floor and slapped his face. Billy pulled a revolver and shot the man dead. Before he could be arrested the Kid ran off to New Mexico and holed up for the winter.

In the spring he took a job cowboying for rancher John Tunstall. It was the middle of a range war and a gang of hired killers rode in and shot down Tunstall. The Kid swore vengeance and killed everyone he believed had had a hand in the killing, including a sheriff and his deputy. Afterward he surrendered to the authorities.

In jail, Billy began to have doubts about his chances to receive a fair trial. He escaped and joined forces with a band of outlaws. He shot his way out of a trap set by lawman Pat Garrett. Garrett's posse stayed on his track and the Kid surrendered to them and was jailed. Four months later he killed two guards and escaped into the hills.

The Kid hid out at a sheep camp near Fort Sumner, New Mexico but eventually ventured into town to see a girlfriend. Pat Garrett was waiting for him there, sitting on the edge of the bed in the dark. He shot the Kid through the heart.

The short, turbulent life of Billy the Kid, age 21, had come to a tragic end. He had been a gunfighter for less than four years and killed a half-dozen men. Over time his exploits became exaggerated and sensationalized and Billy the Kid became one of the West's most enduring and colorful outlaw legends.

WYATT EARP

Like many western gunfighters Wyatt Earp operated on both sides of the law.

He was born in Illinois and moved with his family to California. In his early 20s Wyatt worked his way east to Missouri where he worked for the railroad as a section hand and later as a buffalo hunter. He was arrested in Indian Territory for horse rustling and when released he moved from one town to the next, earning his living as a gambler.

In 1875 Wyatt became a law officer in Wichita, Kansas but he was arrested for fighting, kicked off the force and run out of town. He traveled west to Dodge City and was assistant marshal before drifting through New Mexico, Texas, and finally Tombstone, Arizona where he became deputy sheriff. He acquired an interest in the Oriental Saloon and it was said he was trying to muscle his way into the local rustling and stage robbing activity. Some feel this competition led to a feud that climaxed in the bloody battle at the O.K. Corral.

After the shootout Wyatt moved to San Francisco and married for the third time. He and his wife moved to Colorado, Kansas and then to the Idaho gold fields. He spent time in Nome where he operated the Dexter Saloon during the Alaskan gold rush. Returning to the states Wyatt and his wife prospected in the Southwest and opened yet another saloon in Tonopah, Nevada before finally settling permanently in Los Angeles.

Wyatt spent the rest of his life involved in real estate deals and some said he skillfully operated a series of confidence games. He worked tirelessly, but with little success, to publicize his adventures in books and movies. He died in 1929 at the age of 80, with his boots off. In death he attained the notoriety and fame that had eluded him during his lifetime.

KING OF THE RUSTLERS

Nate Champion was born into a well-known Texas family. He might have stayed home and become a respected rancher but he chose the life of a free-roaming cowboy.

At the age of 24 Nate joined a cattle drive. When it reached Wyoming he decided to stay and found the established ranchers were battling homesteaders for control of the range. Nate did not approve of the way the wealthy cattlemen operated, hiring Regulators to run homesteaders off their land and killing anyone who stood in their way.

Nate began appropriating stray cattle from the large ranchers, driving them away from the area and selling them. His reputation became legendary. He was proclaimed "King of the Rustlers".

The Regulators had standing orders to shoot Nate on sight and in the fall of 1891 they nearly succeeded. Nate was living in a remote line shack along the Powder River. Early one morning four members of the Regulators kicked in the door and one of the gunfighters shouted, "Give up! We've got you this time."

Nate calmly asked, "What's the matter, boys?" and then yanked loose his six-guns from their holsters on the bedpost. In a roar of gunfire one of his assailants was struck in the arm and another in the side. All four intruders ran to the door and high-tailed it for the hills.

The following year Nate was in the Hole-In-The-Wall country. Fifty Regulators surrounded his cabin, set a wagon loaded with hay on fire and pushed it against the cabin wall. Nate came out with his six-guns blazing. The Regulators shot him down and continued to pump lead into him to make sure he was dead; he was shot 28 times. Two weeks later his remains were retrieved and the homesteaders buried him as a martyred hero in the small cemetery in Buffalo, Wyoming.

VIGILANTE JUSTICE

Henry Plummer, impressed with stories from the gold fields, ran away from his Connecticut home when he was 15. He had one thought in his mind -- to strike it rich.

In Nevada City, California the young man discovered there were no easy pickings and decided to make his fortune a different way. He took to gambling and in 1856 the nineteen-year-old was elected the town marshal, a position he held until the day a miner came home and discovered his wife in the marshal's embrace. There was an argument and Plummer shot the miner dead.

The young man fled north, became a suspect in the shooting of a lawman in Oregon and turned up in the boomtown of Lewiston, Idaho where he again became involved in gambling and made himself the leader of a band of highwaymen.

He moved his operations to Bannack, Montana where his company of desperadoes preyed upon miners, travelers, stagecoaches and gold shipments. His gang called themselves the Innocents and identified each other with secret handshakes and special kerchief knots. They marked stagecoaches with coded symbols, indicating which had valuables and were to be robbed.

Plummer ambushed the town marshal and pinned the star to his own chest. But a group of locals formed a vigilante organization and within a month, 20 of Plummer's gang were shot or hanged.

Plummer himself was taken into custody and thrown into his own jail. Though he begged for mercy a lynch mob broke into the jail, carried Plummer to a make-shift gallows and, without wasting time for a trial, they pronounced him guilty and hung him.

INDIAN KILLER

Twin brothers, Sam and Harry Lockhart, were among the early settlers in Northern California. The local Indians, the Pit River tribe, resented the intrusion of the white men and in January 1857 they attacked the small settlement of Shasta and massacred every person they could find.

Sam Lockhart was away at the time but when he returned and discovered his brother had been killed, he swore undying vengeance against all Indians. He took to the hills and every Indian he came across he acted as judge, jury and executioner.

Several times federal authorities warned Sam about his indiscriminate killing of Indians and several times he was arrested. But as soon as he was released he would return to his killing ways. By his own estimates he killed 25 Indians before he felt his brother's death had been avenged.

By then gold had been discovered in Idaho and Sam moved on to Silver City where he took a mining claim. It was here, on the evening of April 1, 1868, that Sam and a fellow miner, Marion Moore, argued over the boundary between their mining claims. Both men went for their guns.

Moore was struck by a bullet in the chest, he staggered a few feet and fell face forward in the mud. He was dead. Sam was wounded in the left arm but claimed he had only been winged and invited his friends to accompany him to the saloon for a drink of whiskey.

A few days later the doctor was called. By then gangrene had set in and Sam's arm had to be amputated. The operation was followed by blood poisoning and Sam suffered terribly. In his delirium he ranted and raved in graphic detail about each Indian he had killed until mercifully, on the 13th day of July, the troubled life of Sam Lockhart came to an end.

BLACK BART

Black Bart was one of the most successful outlaws in the history of the far West. During his eight-year reign, he was credited with robbing 28 stages.

It all began the summer of 1875. A lone gunman stepped into the road at the top of a long, steep grade, leveled a shotgun at the driver and told him, "This is a holdup!"

Later, in town, the driver claimed that the robber "seemed like a real gentleman. He told me he meant me no harm, even cracked a few jokes. He was wearing a long linen duster, a flour sack over his face with eye-holes, and a derby hat. He used a double-barreled shotgun and escaped on foot. I'm afraid that's about all I can tell you."

On the fourth robbery the hold-up man left behind a poem in the empty strong box. It was signed, "Black Bart". From then on, throughout California and southern Oregon, Black Bart marked each robbery with a colorful poem.

The beginning of the end for Black Bart came during a robbery. A passenger tossed a weapon to the stage driver who fired three quick rounds and, though Black Bart managed to escape, he left behind a pair of field glasses, his derby hat and a handkerchief. The handkerchief proved the most damaging. It bore a laundry mark, FX07. Detectives searched the Chinese laundries in San Francisco and learned the mark belonged to C.E. Bolton, alias for Charles Boles.

Boles was tricked into coming to the Wells Fargo office. He strolled in with all the trappings of a gentleman; a gilded walking stick, a diamond ring on his finger, a diamond tie tack, a heavy gold watch fob and an expensive derby hat set at a rakish angle. When he realized he had been discovered he agreed to confess. In return Black Bart was given a relatively light sentence, six years at San Quentin. He was released early on good behavior.

FINAL INSULT

Adam Wimple drifted into the Oregon Territory in the 1840s. He was a man without a past and was soon to be a man without a future.

Wimple, who was about 35 years old at the time, married a 13-year-old girl named Mary and they took up residence near the town of Dallas. A few months after the wedding a neighboring couple stopped for a visit but Wimple told them, "Mary ain't feelin' well this mornin'." The couple left and traveled about a mile when they looked behind them and saw smoke. They hurried back to the Wimple place to find the house engulfed in flames. When the fire burned out the remains of Mary were found under the floor.

Wimple was soon captured and brought to Dallas. When asked why he had killed Mary he said, "Well, I killed her. I don't know why."

Since there was no jail, sheriff Frank Nichols took Wimple to his house. Guards were assigned around the clock to watch the prisoner but Wimple managed to escape. He was tracked through the woods and recaptured standing in the ashes where his house had been.

A trial was held and Wimple was found guilty of murder in the first degree. He was sentenced to hang. On the way to the gallows Wimple sat on his coffin in the bed of the wagon. They met the sheriff's father, Ben Nichols, on the road and Wimple inquired of him, "Ben, you're headed in the wrong direction. Ain't you goin' to the hangin'? Don't you wanna see me hang?"

Ben touched spurs to his mount and as he passed the wagon he rebuffed Wimple with, "I've seen enough of you. I don't wanna see you no more."

MARTHA JANE

Martha Jane Canarray was born in Missouri and lived an uneventful childhood until the family moved west in a covered wagon and settled in the booming mining town of Virginia City, Montana. It was here the young woman encountered the wild side of life.

Martha Jane became acquainted with saloons and would watch the goings-on from under the swinging doors. In time she discovered that, with her hair tucked under a hat and wearing her father's trousers, she could walk into any saloon.

She ran away from home and took to the life of a cowboy. She drove cattle, rounded up wild horses and even worked as a miner mucking ore with a pick and shovel. She acted like a man, dressed like a man, drank and cussed like a man and wore a .45 Colt on her hip. In 1875 she was hired as an Indian scout for General Crook.

A few years later, having heard of the success of Buffalo Bill's touring wild west show, she put together her own company and entertained eastern crowds with her shooting ability and the flavor of the rip-roaring western life. But her status as a star could not insulate her. It seemed that whenever she got liquored up trouble found her. At nearly every city on the tour she had difficulty with the law and finally she retired from public life.

She spent her last years near Deadwood, South Dakota where she sold out-of-towners a small, two-bit autobiography of her exploits. On her deathbed she asked to be buried next to legendary gunfighter Wild Bill Hickok.

On August 2, 1903 the request was granted and the woman known as Calamity Jane was laid to rest beside the man she professed to love.

DARING ROBBERY

On the last day of January 1874, just before the southbound express was scheduled to reach Gads Hill, Missouri, five mounted men appeared at the edge of town. They rode to the depot where one of the men dismounted and threw a switch. Another rode up the track and began waving a red flag.

The engineer of the approaching train saw him, threw on the brakes and the engine careened onto the siding amid a shower of sparks. It came to a screeching stop only a few feet from the Gads Hill sawmill. The conductor, wanting to know what the trouble was, jumped down and was met by hooded men with guns drawn.

A railroad agent ordered the porter to lock the doors but the passengers protested. They insisted the doors be unlocked rather than blown off their hinges.

The robbers entered the first-class coach. One of them spoke. "Don't worry, we're only stealing from plug hat gentlemen. All of you who work for a living can keep your hard-earned money. I can tell who works. The soft-handed ones are capitalists. They take money from me and you."

The train was sided for nearly an hour while the robbers selectively stole from the passengers and ransacked the baggage car and the safe. As they remounted their horses, one of the men handed a note to the conductor and told him, "Give this to the newspaper."

The note was a press release with the headline proclaiming, "THE MOST DARING ROBBERY ON RECORD," and giving all the details of the bold train robbery. The handwriting proved to be that of the notorious outlaw Jesse James.

THE HANGING

"I was visiting my grandmother when word came around that Daniel Delaney had been murdered," recalled Kate Miller. "That was in January of 1865.

"Even though I was quite young I was acquainted with Mr. Delaney because in those days folks would stop and visit with neighbors anytime you passed their homesteads.

"Mr. Delaney had come to Oregon with the first wagon train that ever crossed the plains. He took a land claim south of Salem and as far as I know he was a lone man without a family. He was quite elderly, at least 70 years old.

"There was no crime to speak of back then and that was what made it so difficult to conceive of the fact anyone would kill Mr. Delaney. But kill him they did.

"Some months later, while I was walking to school in Salem with some of my girl friends, we saw men building a platform. We asked them what they were doing and they related they were building a gallows from which two men, Baker and Beale, were to hang for killing Mr. Delaney. We hurried away as fast as we could go.

"The execution was to be a public event and as the date drew near it became the talk of the Willamette Valley. Folks were abuzz and the excitement became so intense some drove 20 miles with kids piled in the back of their wagons.

"I never even considered attending the hanging myself. The thought of doing so, quite frankly, turned my stomach. But I did go close enough to see the crowd assembled along Mill Creek. It was a big crowd, as big as a circus would have commanded only, as it turned out, this crowd sought their entertainment in a very strange and morbid way."

THE SHORT LIFE

Luke Short, one of the legendary gunfighters of the wild West, was born in Mississippi about 1854 and grew up on a west Texas ranch. He left home at a young age and worked for a while as a cowboy. Later he discovered he had a lucky flair and began drifting from one settlement to the next engaging cowboys, miners and professional gamblers in games of chance.

During those early days he sharpened his gunslinging skills, practicing several hours a day on the quickness of his draw and shooting accuracy. His first test was during a card game at the Oriental Saloon in Tombstone, Arizona. Charlie Storms, a dangerous character, did not like the way his luck was running. He leaped to his feet, pushed over the table and accused Luke of cheating.

"Any time you're ready," Luke said with cold confidence. Charlie went for his revolver but before he cleared leather Luke had drawn and fired. Charlie was the first of many who would die at the quick hands of Luke Short.

Luke traveled north, landing in Dodge City where he bought an interest in the Long Branch Saloon. He hired a pretty girl to play the piano but his competition took exception to this and forced the passage of an ordinance that outlawed any performance by female piano players.

Luke vowed to fight. He wired friends Bat Masterson and Wyatt Earp, asking for their help. They arrived and within the hour the ordinance had been reversed and the Long Branch was back in business with the pretty performer as the featured attraction.

Luke always figured he would die as violently as he had lived. But such was not the case. One day out of the blue he became ill and died in bed soon after. He was 39 years old.

BLOODY REVENGE

Hugh Anderson helped push a herd of longhorn cattle from Texas to the railhead in Newton, Kansas. It was here, at the end of the long drive, that his troubles began.

A friend of Anderson's was killed during a card game and Anderson swore to avenge his death. In a bloody barroom gun battle the killer, Mike McCluskie, was sent to meet his maker. Anderson barely escaped town with his life.

Two years later Anderson was tending bar at the Trading Post in Medicine Lodge, Kansas. A man came in and announced that Mike McCluskie's brother Arthur was in town seeking vengeance. Anderson said he would meet McCluskie in the street and closed the bar.

Outside a boisterous crowd was betting on the outcome while the two adversaries positioned themselves twenty paces apart, backs to each other. A signal shot was fired. Each man whirled, drew, fired.

McCluskie's second shot slammed into Anderson's arm and he crumpled to his knees but recovered enough to send a bullet into McCluskie's face. The big man roared in pain and spit out blood and chunks of bone and teeth. Anderson kept pulling the trigger. McCluskie was hit in the leg and the chest but as he went down he got off a shot striking Anderson in the stomach and sending him over onto his back.

McCluskie pulled his knife and began crawling toward his enemy. A few members of the crowd called out to stop the pathetic contest but they were rebuffed. "They'll fight 'till they die. Them's the rules."

As McCluskie inched forward Anderson struggled to sit. He drew his knife and waited. When McCluskie was nearly upon him he lashed out, slashing McCluskie's neck. McCluskie managed to stab Anderson in the side. The sun tumbled from the sky and the blood of the two adversaries mixed together and sank into the sand.

THE DESPERADO LAWMAN

Missouri-born Henry Brown was orphaned and at an early age took up the life of a wandering cowboy. He worked on ranches in Kansas and Colorado and then signed on with a cattle drive in the Texas panhandle. One night on the trail the normally quiet young man quarreled with another cowboy. Angry words were exchanged, followed by three quick shots and Brown's rival lay dead.

With that killing the young cowboy entered a life of crime. He joined Billy The Kid and his gang of outlaws. He was in a big shootout in Lincoln, New Mexico and escaped by vaulting over an eight-foot wall.

After that narrow escape he supposedly changed his desperado ways. In 1882 Brown was appointed marshal of Caldwell, Kansas, a wild settlement on the cattle trail from Texas. Brown and his deputy, Ben Wheeler, took control and drove the criminal element out of town, leaving the door wide open for themselves.

On April 30, 1884 Brown and Wheeler announced they would be out of town a few days searching for a murderer. They were joined by two men and together they traveled 75 miles in a driving rainstorm to Medicine Lodge, Kansas. They rode directly to the Medicine Valley Bank and demanded money. The cashier reached for his revolver and Brown shot him dead. The bank president was shot but managed to stagger to the safe and throw the lock.

The robbers escaped empty-handed, pursued by an angry posse. Brown and his gang were trapped in a box canyon and forced to surrender. They were brought back to town and held in a make-shift jail. That evening a lynch mob overpowered the guard and dragged the bank robbers into the street. Brown tried to run and was cut down with a blast from a shotgun. The other three robbers were hoisted into the air and danced at the end of a rope.

LAWMAN'S SECRET

Frank Canton is best known as a lawman who helped to tame the wild West. He was elected sheriff of Johnson County, Wyoming; undersheriff of Pawnee County, Oklahoma Territory; and, for a time, rode tall in the saddle as a United States Marshal. In the 1890s he followed the gold rush to the Klondike and was a deputy marshal in Alaska.

It was not until after his death, at the age of 78, that the true identity and the many secrets of the famous lawman were revealed. His name was Joseph Horner. He was born in 1849, the son of a Virginia doctor. After the Civil War the family moved to Texas.

It was never revealed what led the boy to turn to crime but by the time he was in his early 20s he was wanted for a string of bank robberies, assaults and cattle rustling. His hell-raising finally culminated in a saloon brawl with a group of United States cavalrymen. He drew his six-shooter and killed one of the soldiers and then shot his way out of town. After that he departed Texas, took the name Frank Canton, and began his new life on the side of law and order.

Years later, his health failing, the famous lawman returned to Texas to make peace with the ghosts of his past. He met with the governor, confessed to the crimes of his youth and asked forgiveness. The governor pardoned him and suggested, "Why don't you stay in Texas and resume your true identity?"

"Can't," said the old man. "I want to be remembered for the good things I've done, not the bad. I'll be Frank Canton, lawman, until the day I die."

THE DRUNKEN POSSE

"The story I am about to relate occurred one summer night in the year 18 and 84," told stage driver Tom Burnett. "There was a bright moon and just as the stage reached a clump of trees two men stepped into the road. One had a six-shooter and the other a shotgun.

"'Get your hands up!' barked the fellow with the shotgun.

I slowly raised my hands, with the lines in them, as high as my shoulders. While the man with the shotgun kept it trained on me, the other one went to the stage door and ordered everyone out. I leaned over and said, 'Say, Partner, no use making the women get out. They haven't any money and are probably scared to death.'

"He said the women could stay. There was only one man passenger and he was a preacher. He handed over his money and the robber grumbled because it was only three dollars. Meanwhile the man with the shotgun had me toss down the Wells Fargo treasure chest and the registered mail. There was a little over $7,000 in the treasure chest.

"I drove to the end of my run and reported the robbery. A posse was organized. Some of the men had been drinking pretty heavily and consequently they were a noisy bunch.

"As it turned out, the robbers were on foot and as the posse approached, whooping and hollering, the outlaws concluded it was nothing more than a crowd of drunken farmers coming back from a dance. Consequently, they stayed on the road and were apprehended by the posse who found their pockets stuffed with stolen loot. The robbers stood trial, were found guilty and spent seven years in the state penitentiary.

WILD BILL

At an early age James Butler Hickok distinguished himself as the best shot in northern Illinois. He was hired as a Union wagon master during the Civil War and once, when he backed down a lynch mob, a woman shouted out, "Good for you, Wild Bill!" The nickname stuck.

After the war Wild Bill was a scout for Custer's 7th Cavalry and later became a deputy U.S. marshal, making a name for himself when he and Buffalo Bill Cody brought in eleven prisoners. He was sheriff of Hays City, Kansas and city marshal of Abilene, Kansas.

In Abilene he became involved in a gun battle in the Bull's Head Saloon. Deputy Mike Williams broke through the crowd hoping to assist the marshal. Surrounded by a hostile crowd Wild Bill saw movement, whirled and fired, killing his own deputy. Following this tragedy Wild Bill, who was credited with killing seven men, is said to have sworn he would never fire his weapon again.

For a time Wild Bill toured with Buffalo Bill Cody's Wild West Show but he was not much of a performer and the make-believe life was not to his liking. The summer of 1876 found Wild Bill in the booming gold town of Deadwood, Dakota Territory where he spent most of his time gambling.

On the afternoon of August 2nd, Wild Bill entered a card game at Saloon No. 10. Within a half hour he had lost his money and requested a $50 stake from the house to stay in the game. Ten minutes after four o'clock Jack McCall, who had lost to Wild Bill the night before, tossed down a glass of whiskey, drew his .45 Colt and shot Wild Bill in the back of the head. Wild Bill fell to the floor dead, clutching his cards; a queen and two pairs, aces over eights.

McCall was tried, convicted and hung. Wild Bill's possessions were raffled off to pay his funeral expenses and he was buried owing a debt of $50 to the house.

OWE YOU ONE

Walter Catron, a resident of northeastern Oregon, was herding sheep in Joseph Canyon that warm spring day in 1914, the day of his terrible accident.

He packed a rifle to protect himself and defend his flock from bears and cougars. As he went to slip it in the saddle scabbard the trigger hung up on something and the rifle fired. Walter was knocked to the ground. The bullet had entered his right leg near the front pocket and traveled a ways before exiting and striking his left leg between the knee and hip.

The injured man tore his shirt into strips and tried to stem the flow of blood with compresses. He knew his only chance was to ride up and out of the canyon to Doc Gilmore in the settlement of Flora, ten miles away. He gritted his teeth against the searing pain and pulled himself onto the saddle. He told his horse, "Let's go, boy. Get me out of here."

On top was a gate. By the time his horse reached that point Walter was lightheaded and sick to his stomach from loss of blood and shock. He reached down and pulled his damaged right leg up and over, twisted onto his belly and let himself down, using one hand on the saddle horn and the other on the cantle.

His legs would not hold him and he collapsed with a cry of pain. He lay there for a long moment before recovering enough to crawl to the gate and pull himself up. With a herculean effort he managed to open the gate. But when he tried to remount he could not.

It was at that point that Warren McWillett, a homesteader in the area, arrived at the gate. He found Walter, boosted him onto his horse and lead the way to town.

After he was sufficiently healed Walter swung by Warren's homestead and told him, "Thanks for saving my life. I owe you one."

THE DARK SIDE

Clay Allison grew up on his family's farm in Tennessee. He fought for the Confederacy and after the close of the Civil War he drifted to Texas and became a cowhand, helping blaze the famous Goodnight-Loving Trail and riding on many cattle drives. He was a trusted cowhand but when he drank alcohol, a dark side of his personality emerged.

It was believed Clay whet his appetite for killing as a member of a drunken lynch mob. Then he killed a man in a gunfight and was suspected of dry-gulching another.

The Clay Allison legend grew. A story circulated that Clay challenged a man to a knife fight in an open grave, saying, "It'll save the trouble of buryin' the loser." Spectators claimed it was a grisly affair and that Clay climbed from the hole dripping blood from many wounds, laughing insanely and went directly to the nearest saloon for a drink.

Another story claimed that in the Wyoming Territory he developed a severe toothache. He rode to Cheyenne and requested a dentist to pull the tooth. The dentist extracted the wrong one and this so enraged Clay that he strapped the dentist into his own chair and pulled one of the unfortunate man's front teeth.

Just before Christmas 1876, Clay killed a deputy sheriff at the Olympic Dance Hall in Las Animas, Colorado. He stood trial but the jury, afraid of the gunman's reputation, turned him free.

The violent life of Clay Allison ended near Pecos, Texas. He was horseback and overtook a freighter having trouble with his horses on a steep grade. Clay offered to drive the unruly team to the bottom of the hill. The teamster quickly accepted. On the descent the horses began running, the wagon struck a rock and Clay was hurled to the ground where a wheel of the heavily-laden wagon fractured his skull.

RIVER GHOST

The question remains to this day -- was James White the first white man to pass through the Grand Canyon, or was he nothing more than a gunslinging murderer?

The few facts center around Callville, Nevada, at that time the head of navigation on the Colorado River. On September 8, 1867 a group of workers was loading a cargo of rock salt on a barge. One of the men suddenly pointed upriver and shouted, "What's that?"

In midstream was a log raft and a nearly naked man. The workers carried the man out of the heat. He was in dreadful shape; mumbling incoherently, dehydrated, nearly starved and his skin blistered from the sun.

The man, who whispered that his name was James White, began to tell an incredible tale. He said he and two other prospectors had been attacked by Indians. One was killed outright and White and the other man had managed to escape into the canyon carved by the Colorado River. They built a raft and set off downstream. On the third day White's companion drowned. After another 11 days of battling dangerous whirlpools and towering whitewater the raft had floated free of the Grand Canyon.

For a time White's story went unchallenged but as others explored the Grand Canyon doubts were raised. Rivermen wanted to know how White had navigated 500 miles of wild water in only 14 days. The physical descriptions of the canyon that White gave did not match. Finally White's character was called into question. Circumstantial evidence suggested he had killed his partners and made up his epic tale.

None of the fragmentary clues ever proved White had purposely lied and a motive for murder was never established. White maintained his innocence to the end of his days. And the Colorado never gave up its ghosts.

FRANK JAMES

Frank James, the eldest son of a frontier preacher, veered from the straight-and-narrow path and, with his younger brother Jesse, became one of the west's most notorious outlaws.

Frank was born in 1843 in Clay County, Missouri and joined the Confederacy as a member of Quantrill's infamous band of Missouri raiders. After the war Frank, Jesse and the Younger brothers were involved in numerous bank holdups and train robberies. The gang wore masks so it was difficult to assign blame or give credit for all the crimes they might have committed.

In 1876 Frank married a Kansas girl, Annie Ralston. That same year the James-Younger gang was decimated after a failed bank robbery in Northfield, Minnesota. Frank and Jesse hid out in Tennessee for a time before returning to Missouri.

The outlaw ways of the James brothers ended when Jesse was gunned down in 1882. Frank surrendered to Missouri Governor Thomas Crittendon, the man responsible for having Jesse killed. Years of trials, appeals and legal maneuvering resulted in Frank's release in 1885. For the next 30 years he lived a quiet and an honest existence living in New Jersey, Texas, Oklahoma, Louisiana and Missouri.

Frank drifted from one job to the next. He was the doorman at a St. Louis burlesque. He traveled to county fairs around the country, firing his famous pistol to start horse races. He played on his reputation as an outlaw and became a partner in a traveling James-Younger Wild West Show.

Frank James died at his mother's farm in Missouri in 1915. His ashes were kept in a bank vault for nearly 30 years until his wife's death when their ashes were interred together in a Kansas City cemetery.

THE HOLD-UP

"Was I ever held up? You bet I was," stated veteran stage driver Cal Scovill. "One time I was carrying a big shipment of gold in the Wells Fargo treasure chest. The company was taking no chances -- they sent along a guard armed with a sawed-off shotgun.

"The run was quiet until all of a sudden a road agent stepped out from behind a tree and got the drop on us. He barked at me to heave out the treasure chest. You could tell he was a young man from his voice, but a mask covered his face. All I could do was obey. Then he ordered me to drive away and not look back.

"'Drive, don't stop!' the guard whispered to me. 'Circle back through the timber. I'll drop off. Maybe I can get a shot.'

"I drove on and a few minutes later there came a loud report. I figured the guard had slipped up on the masked man as he was busy trying to break the lock on the treasure chest. That's the way I had it figured.

"I continued on to a wide spot in the road, turned around and drove back to the scene of the hold-up. Sure enough, there lay the treasure chest in the middle of the road and slumped over it was the body of the road agent. He had been shot in the back. Nearby, crying as if his heart would break, was the Wells Fargo guard.

"'You got your man. He was the one that did it. What's there to cry about?' I called.

"The guard looked up at me and if I live to be a hundred I will never forget the expression of agony and sadness etched into his face. He spoke to me, 'Cal, I've just killed my own son.'"

BEN THOMPSON

Ben Thompson's first shootout happened when he was only 16. That day he was hunting geese along the Colorado River with friends. Another hunting party was across the river. A flock of geese flew over and when shots were fired before the birds were within range, Ben challenged the leader of the other group to meet in a duel. At forty paces the boys faced off and fired their shotguns at each other. Ben was hit but able to limp away. His opponent had to be carried home.

Ben worked as an apprentice in a print shop until the lure of easy money and a carefree life turned him into a gambler. He drifted to Louisiana, Mexico and Kansas with trouble dogging him at each stop. He killed a Mexican police officer in a quarrel over a senorita. He killed a man over a gambling debt. Another time he shot a man because the man playfully knocked his hat off.

In spite of the fact that Ben Thompson had a short fuse and a fast draw, or maybe because of it, he was elected the marshal of Austin, Texas in 1881. He proved to be an excellent peace officer until the day he gunned down Jack Harris over an old gambling debt. He resigned as marshal, stood trial and was acquitted. After his resignation he began to drink heavily and was involved in several disturbances.

On the evening of March 11, 1884 Ben and a friend, gunfighter King Fisher, were drinking at the Variety Theatre, the same place where Ben had killed Jack Harris. Several patrons had been friends of Harris, a dispute arose and guns were drawn. When the smoke from the ambush cleared, Ben Thompson and King Fisher lay dead, their bodies riddled with 22 wounds.

THE RELUCTANT LAWMAN

When 14-year-old John Hughes left his parents' home in Illinois all he had to his name was a pony, saddle, bedroll and a hankering to see the West. For six years he lived among the Indians learning their ways.

In 1885 Hughes bought a ranch near Liberty Hill, Texas. One morning he awoke to discover a gang of horse thieves had stolen 18 head from his corral as well as an additional 54 horses from his neighbors. Hughes made the neighbors a proposition: if they would take care of his stock he would chase down the thieves.

Strapping on his pearl-handled Colt .45 Hughes took up the trail. Nearly 1,200 miles and one year later he flushed the rustlers and in the ensuing battle four of the outlaws died and the rest threw their hands in the air.

Returning to his ranch Hughes thought the trouble was over but one day he received a message that a friend of one of the slain outlaws was seeking revenge. Hughes met the man and according to an eyewitness, "Hughes had a draw that was lightning quick. The other fellar never had a chance."

Other attempts were made to ambush Hughes and finally he made the decision to accept a commission as a member of the Texas Rangers. For 28 years he rode as a Texas Ranger. He became friends with Zane Grey, the prominent Western writer, and the author dedicated his book, *The Lone Star Ranger*, to Hughes. That book inspired the idea for what would eventually become *The Lone Ranger* radio and television show.

In 1946 Hughes, 89 years old and in failing health, took his old pearl-handled .45, the famous gun that had helped tame the lawless Southwest, turned it on himself and pulled the trigger.

GOOD GONE BAD

Some knew Burt Alvord as a respected lawman and pillar of the community. Others knew him as a cattle rustler and train robber.

As a teenager Alvord was living in Tombstone, Arizona and was working as a stable hand at the O.K. Corral the day of the famous shootout. He took to the gun to settle his disputes and was 20 years old when he killed his first man.

The following year John Slaughter was elected sheriff of Cochise County and he swore in Alvord as his deputy. Together they brought a semblance of law and order to the wild country. But Alvord began frequenting the bars of Tombstone and eventually the alcohol clouded his judgment. One time he shot and wounded a man during a drunken brawl; another time he had difficulties with a cowboy and emptied his pistol in the man's face.

After that incident Alvord was considered a liability and was forced to resign as deputy. He drifted south to Mexico and turned to rustling cattle. However, he claimed he had come to his senses and had given up drinking. He returned to the right side of the law as the constable of Willcox, Arizona.

It was while he was a respected lawman that he used his position to mastermind and execute a series of daring train robberies. He was arrested in 1900, stood trial and was convicted. He escaped from jail in 1903 and concocted an elaborate plot to fake his death; even having a coffin sent to Tombstone with instructions for his burial. But the ruse was discovered, Alvord was recaptured and spent two years in prison at Yuma, Arizona. When released he left the country and traveled to Latin America where he worked, for a time, as a laborer on the Panama Canal. He died in 1910.

WHITE HORSE BLACK HORSE

Fred Inkleman worked on a ranch in the Baker Valley of northeastern Oregon. He argued with the rancher over wages and the next day he stole ten of the rancher's horses, including several Percherons imported from France and valued at $1,000 a head. That night he set camp at the edge of Sumpter Valley near the homestead cabin of John Duckworth.

Duckworth related the following story: "It all began at daybreak with a string of gunshots. A few minutes later I spotted a white horse that I recognized belonged to my neighbor, Mr. Allen. It was bleeding from a wound.

"I backtracked the horse and soon found the body of Mr. Allen. There were other tracks and upon following these I found a black horse and the body of another neighbor, Mr. Rivers. The two men had gone hunting together that morning.

"Presently the sheriff and his deputy from Baker City rode up. They said they were on the trail of a horse thief. What struck me as strange was the fact the sheriff was riding a black horse and his deputy a white horse.

"They took up the trail of the stolen horses and at long last the lawmen overtook a wagon freighter. They asked the teamster if he had seen a lone rider pushing a herd of Percheron horses and he replied, 'He's coming down the ridge right now.'

"The lawmen got the drop on Inkleman. At his trial, when asked why he had killed Allen and Rivers, he shrugged and said, 'I knew the sheriff in this part of the country rode a black and the deputy rode a white horse. I wasn't takin' chances.'

"The jury found Inkleman guilty and he was sentenced to life in prison. But he ended up dying of a gangrene infection in his leg and so a violent end came to the violent life of a murderer who was but 19 years old."

BLOOD ALLEY

For years the Dalton gang terrorized Oklahoma and Kansas. No bank, train or stage was safe. But all that changed in the bloodbath of October 5, 1892. On that date the Dalton gang had planned their most daring robbery, holding up two banks at once in Coffeyville, Kansas.

The gang tied their horses in an alley near the two banks. Brothers Bob and Emmett Dalton stepped into the First National Bank, held guns on the cashier and customers and scooped $21,000 into a grain sack. As they emerged through the front door they were met with a hail of gunfire from townspeople who had recognized the gang riding into town. The Daltons ducked back inside and tried to flee through the back door. One man blocked their path and he was gunned down. Two more men appeared and were shot. A fourth man fell victim to the Daltons as they fled to the alley.

At the same time, across the street in the Condon Bank, the other members of the gang, Bill Powers, Dick Broadwell, and brother Grat Dalton, had managed to grab $1,500 and escape. They also ran to the alley. Confusion reigned as the gang tried to mount. A barrage of gunfire killed two horses and then Bob Dalton took a slug in the chest. He staggered back, sat down and died.

Grat killed the town marshal before he took a slug in the neck. Powers and Broadwell were shot down. Emmett Dalton grabbed his horse and swung on board but a shotgun blasted him out of the saddle.

While the bodies of the Dalton gang were propped up and photographed, Emmett, the only member to survive what became known as the "Shootout in Blood Alley", was carried to the Farmer's Hotel. He was nursed back to health by his mother and lived a long life, dying in 1937 of natural causes.

DIAMONDFIELD JACK

Jack Davis was known throughout the far West by the name "Diamondfield Jack". He was given that alias because he often bragged he knew of a place where diamonds could be found lying on top of the ground. For proof he showed off his sparkling diamond stick pin. Besides being a big talker, he also had a mean reputation as a gunfighter.

It was said that Diamondfield Jack had been hired by cattlemen to intimidate the sheepmen and make them leave the open range. In 1896 two sheepherders in Cassia County, Idaho were found shot to death and the finger of guilt pointed toward Diamondfield Jack. He was arrested and charged with two counts of murder.

At his trial several sheepherders testified that Jack had threatened to kill them if they did not voluntarily leave the country. Tests proved Jack's gun was not the murder weapon and a witness testified Jack had been in Nevada at the time of the killing. Nevada Governor Sparks, who had once employed Jack, swore under oath that the accused was an honest, hard-working man incapable of cold-blooded murder. The jury, paying no attention to the evidence, found Jack guilty. He was sentenced to hang.

Hanging Diamondfield Jack proved difficult. A rider galloped into town with a postponement. There was a second postponement and finally, just before Jack was to be led to the gallows for the third time, two ranchers came forward and confessed to killing the sheepherders. They were acquitted when it was ruled they had acted in self-defense.

Diamondfield Jack was released and he promptly left Idaho. He surfaced in Nevada and lived a life of luxury until, in 1949, the gunfighter was accidently run over and killed by a taxi cab.

WES HARDIN

John Wesley Hardin was expected to follow in his father's footsteps as a circuit-riding preacher in Texas. But he took up with the devil instead and became one of the most feared gunfighters in the history of the West.

Hardin's career began at the early age of 11 when he drew a knife during a quarrel and stabbed a boy in the chest. That boy lived, but a few years later Hardin killed his first man, a former slave, with three shots from his .44. When three soldiers came to arrest him he ambushed them, killing two with a shotgun and the third with his six-shooter.

After several more killings and with a $4,000 dead-or-alive reward on his head, Hardin fled to Florida. He was buying and selling cattle and horses when Texas Rangers hunted him down and returned him to Texas to stand trial. He was sentenced to the penitentiary and spent his time studying law books. He was released in 1894 and opened a law office but soon began running with a hard crowd in the notorious border town of El Paso.

On the evening of August 19, 1895 Hardin was drinking and gambling at the Acme Saloon, shooting dice with a local grocer. He had just rolled the dice and announced loudly, "You have four sixes to beat".

At that point John Selman, Sr., entered the establishment. He was a peace officer who had quarreled with Hardin in the past. Selman later claimed that he had spoken a word of warning, that Hardin had turned and gone for his guns. Eyewitnesses disputed this claim. At any rate Selman shot Hardin in the head and, after he fell to the ground, pumped two more slugs into the lifeless body. Selman stood trial but was acquitted.

Wes Hardin, 42 years old, the man who had been in at least 19 gunfights and killed 11 men, died as he had lived -- by the gun.

LONGHAIRED JIM

"Longhaired Jim" Courtright was born in Iowa, served as a Union soldier during the Civil War and showed up afterward in Texas as an Army scout. In 1876 he was appointed city marshal of Fort Worth. Three years later he drifted to New Mexico and was hired by his former commanding officer, Union General John "Black Jack" Logan, as ranch foreman of Logan's New Mexico holdings. His main duty was to keep the range clear of rustlers, sodbusters and squatters.

In 1883 Courtright came across two men who had taken up residence on the range and were claiming the land. The foreman ordered them to leave and when they refused, gunplay broke out. Both squatters were shot to death. To avoid trial Courtright fled to Fort Worth and opened a private detective firm. When extradition papers were served he bolted to Canada but eventually came back to New Mexico and cleared his name.

He returned to Fort Worth and his detective firm, which was nothing more than a front to provide protection for the town's gambling establishments. Courtright ruled with an iron hand until gunfighter Luke Short arrived in town, purchased a third interest in the White Elephant Saloon and refused to pay protection money.

On February 8, 1887 the two men argued, a gunfight erupted and, though Courtright cleared leather, his gun was shot out of his hand. Of the five remaining bullets that Short fired, three struck Courtright, one finding his heart.

Short was cleared of murder charges on the grounds the killing had been in self-defense.

DOC HOLLIDAY

John Henry Holliday was a gentleman, a dentist from a wealthy Southern family. In 1873 he contracted tuberculosis and was given four years to live.

He headed west to seek a climate which might prolong his life. For a time he practiced dentistry but with nothing to lose he chose a wilder life, becoming a professional gambler and proficient with a pair of pistols. He practiced the fast draw at every opportunity and on January 1, 1875 Holliday exchanged shots with a saloon keeper. Neither party was injured but the reputation of Doc Holliday was born.

Holliday appeared in numerous boom towns across the West - Cheyenne, Wyoming; Dodge City, Kansas; Leadville, Colorado; and Tucson and Tombstone in Arizona. Wherever he went he drank and gambled. He killed a man in New Mexico and shot up a saloon in Tombstone after the saloon keeper accused Doc of participating in a stagecoach robbery. Doc Holliday stood shoulder to shoulder with his friend Marshal Wyatt Earp at the O.K. Corral shootout.

The last gunfight of Doc Holliday's fabled career was in 1884 in Leadville, Colorado against a bartender who made threats about an unpaid gambling loan. Holliday drew his pistol and the bartender turned and ran, tripping in his haste to get away. Holliday put a slug in the man's arm and, for shooting a man while he was down, Doc was taken into custody. He was acquitted.

A year later, suffering from tuberculosis and alcoholism, Holliday traveled to Glenwood Springs, Colorado where he committed himself to a health resort. He died there at the age of 35.

CACHE OF GOLD

Rattlesnake Dick and George Skinner were outlaws who terrorized the border country between Oregon and California. The spring of 1865 found them sharing a campfire.

"Throw in with me and we'll both be rich," promised Rattlesnake Dick.

"How rich?" George Skinner wanted to know.

"Four hundred pounds of gold," claimed Rattlesnake. "We'll split the take."

The plan was for Rattlesnake and another man to steal a pack string of mules from the miners in the settlement of Auburn and to meet up with George and his band of men after they had waylaid the gold shipment. The spot selected for the robbery was high in the Trinity Mountains, where the trail passed along the edge of a sheer drop-off. The heist went according to plan. Skinner and his men made away with the gold. But when they arrived at the rendezvous where Rattlesnake was supposed to meet them with the fresh mules, the meadow was empty.

Rattlesnake and a companion had been captured trying to steal the mules and they were being held in the Auburn jail. Of course, Skinner had no way of knowing this. He waited as long as he dared and then buried half the gold in the woods and loaded the rest on their horses and tried to ride out of the country.

The horses were not up to carrying so much weight and a posse ran them down shortly after they had reached the hideout cave. Skinner tried to escape and was killed. His companions surrendered without a fight.

Half the gold was recovered but, to this day, the remaining 200 pounds of gold remain hidden in a cache somewhere in the mountains along the border between Oregon and California.

BAT MASTERSON

William "Bat" Masterson lived a sheltered life on the family farm in Quebec, but when he was 14 the family moved to a farm near Wichita, Kansas and the boy was introduced to the rough-and-tumble ways of western life.

Bat became a buffalo hunter, killing buffalo for the hides and leaving the meat to rot. He distinguished himself as a skilled gunfighter when he and a small group of hunters fought off an attack by nearly 1,000 Indians.

In 1876, according to legend, Bat was playing cards in a saloon in Mobeetie, Texas. During the evening he became friendly with one of the house girls, Molly Brennan. A soldier from the 4th Cavalry, Sergeant King, took exception to the budding friendship between Bat and Molly. He drew his pistol. When the smoke cleared both Sergeant King and Molly were dead and Bat had taken a slug in his leg. From that day forward he was forced to walk with the aid of a cane.

The following year Bat was elected sheriff of Ford County, Kansas and brought law and order to Dodge City and the surrounding territory. He captured horse thieves, train robbers, murderers, jail escapees and an array of ruffians.

After losing re-election in 1879 Bat drifted through Colorado, New Mexico, Arizona, Texas and Nebraska. As he traveled he began writing stories of his many exploits and selling them to various newspapers. But most of his living was earned as a card shark and later as an official promoter of prizefights and horse races.

In 1891 Bat married and the couple moved to New York City where Bat found employment as a sports writer for the *Morning Telegraph* newspaper. His column won him fame and he became a well-known celebrity around the night spots of New York City. He died at the age of 64 sitting at his desk writing a story.

TRIGGER-HAPPY FOOLS

"Strap on your guns, boys. Meet me on Boot Hill, high noon. One at a time or all together, makes no difference to me," drawled "Turkey Creek" Jack Johnson during a card game argument. The year was 1876. The place Saloon Row, Deadwood, South Dakota.

Johnson was an easy-going sort, a gambler and gunfighter who never lost his temper nor his composure. Whether he was raking in a pot or gunning down a man, he took his time.

The sun was directly overhead and a crowd of onlookers had already gathered when Johnson entered the cemetery from the back side. Straight ahead were the two men Johnson had challenged. In unison they kicked back the tails of their dusters and started moving forward.

Johnson was 50 paces away when one of the men snarled, "Now!" Simultaneously they cleared leather and blazed away. Johnson, cool and calm, kept walking toward them even though dust was kicked up near his feet and hot metal ricocheted, zinging off nearby rocks. He seemed oblivious. He drew his Colt but did not use it, kept coming, one slow step after another. Kept coming.

The two men emptied their revolvers, threw them aside and reached for replacements. The Colt in Johnson's hand suddenly jumped. One of the men gave a sharp grunt, tore at his chest and fell backwards. He was dead.

His partner took a few hesitant steps forward, firing his second pistol wildly in the direction of Johnson. Johnson's stride never varied, slow, steady.... To protect himself the man dropped into a crouch and continued to fire. Three more shots rang out before Johnson ended his life.

After the smoke cleared and the dust had settled Johnson addressed the crowd, "They were nothing but trigger-happy fools. The lesson here - don't let your nerves get the best of you. Take your time. Never be in a hurry to die."

FIRST HOLD-UP

On a cold, rainy Valentine's Day in 1866 a dozen men wearing long Confederate army overcoats and riding spirited horses, swept into the town of Liberty, Missouri. They positioned themselves so they had a commanding view up and down main street.

Two rode to the hitching rail in front of Clay County Savings Bank, dismounted, tied off the reins and stepped through the front door. A father and son operated the bank. They were standing behind the counter when two strangers walked in.

"I wanna change this into something smaller," one of the strangers said and slid a $10 bill across the polished wood. The son glanced down at the bill and up into the gaping muzzle of a six-shooter. A growling voice commanded him, "Changed my mind, give me all the money in the bank."

His partner leveled his revolver at the father and threatened, "Make any problem and I'll shoot you down like a dog." The gunmen left the bank with $60,000 in a grain sack. They directed the father and son to, "Stay put!"

Outside, a 19-year-old student was on his way to class. He was in the wrong place at the wrong time. He stepped off the boardwalk as the outlaws were wildly spurring their mounts up the street. The boy tried to dive out of the way but four shots rang out and he was dead before he hit the ground.

The posse trailed the outlaws as the rain changed to snow. A blizzard blew as darkness fell and the posse gave up.

Years later the James boys, Jesse and Frank - who lived with their mother only a single railroad stop north of Liberty, and their gang were given credit for pulling off the first holdup of a bank, during regular business hours, in the history of the United States.

BILLY CLANTON

Billy Clanton claimed he never wanted trouble with the law but there he was in Tombstone the afternoon of October 26, 1881 staring down the barrel of Morgan Earp's gun.

Billy and his two older brothers had been working with several outlaws rounding up cattle across the border in Mexico and selling them to Arizona ranchers. That day they were about to leave town with a wagon loaded with supplies.

Cutting them off were the Earp brothers, Wyatt, Virgil and Morgan, as well as Doc Holliday. They represented the law in Tombstone and ordered the outlaws to throw down their weapons. Billy Clanton immediately raised his hands and shouted, "Don't shoot! We don't want to fight!"

In response Morgan Earp shoved his six-shooter toward Billy Clanton and fired point blank into the young man's chest. The bullet knocked Billy off his feet and he fell backward clutching at his left breast. For the next half-minute the air was filled with gunfire.

Even though Billy had been wounded in the chest and had his right wrist shattered, he managed to draw his Smith & Wesson revolver with his left hand. Lying on his back, with the gun propped on his knees, he continued firing. Then a final slug struck him in the stomach and all shooting ceased.

Writhing in pain on the ground Billy called out, "Get a doctor." A group picked up the stricken young man and carried him to a nearby building. He spoke in a raspy whisper, "Boys, pull off my boots. I promised my mother I would never die with my boots on."

After he was laid out on the floor, 19-year-old Billy began to cry. He tried to pull himself up, calling out, "They've murdered me!" A doctor arrived and injected him with two syringes of morphine. A few moments later the struggle ended. "Drive the crowd away!" rasped Billy Clanton and promptly died.

RINGO

John Ringo was one of the deadliest gunfighters of his time, but it was his weakness for alcohol that killed him.

Ringo was born in New Jersey and was well-educated. Little else is known about him until he came to Texas and earned a name for himself as a hired gun during a range war. He was quick on the draw and completely fearless in any situation but he was different from others of his kind. He often read from books and when he was drinking, if the mood struck him, he would eloquently quote long verses of poetry or recite passages from Shakespeare.

He visited Tombstone, Arizona and was drawn into a gang of horse and cattle rustlers. Ringo met his end following a drinking escapade with friends Billy Claiborne and "Buckskin Frank" Leslie. When the party broke up the men went their separate ways. The following day Ringo was found beneath a tree in the bottom of Turkey Creek Canyon. It was said his hands and feet had been bound with strips torn from his shirt and that he had been shot and scalped.

Billy Claiborne pointed the finger of guilt at Buckskin Frank. Harsh words were exchanged between the two and Claiborne left the bar where they had been drinking. He concealed himself in a fruit stand overlooking the front door of the saloon. Buckskin Frank anticipated the ambush, crept out the side door, got the drop on Billy and killed him.

Another friend of Ringo's, Pony Deal, accused Johnny O'Rourke of shooting Ringo and killed O'Rourke in revenge. It was never learned who really killed John Ringo.

FLAT NOSE

George "Flat Nose" Curry spent his childhood in Nebraska. At age 15 he went out on his own and began breaking horses. Early in his career as a bronc rider, a wild mustang kicked George in the face producing the anomaly which earned him his nickname.

From breaking horses he went to rustling horses and eventually joined the famous outlaw gang, the Wild Bunch. In 1897 Flat Nose held up a bank in Belle Fourche, South Dakota with the Sundance Kid and Harvey Logan.

Bounty hunters followed them to Montana. A gun battle ensued and Curry was wounded in the arm. The three men were taken into custody and transported to Deadwood to stand trial but they escaped and fled to Nevada.

The next summer Curry and his companions returned east of the Rocky Mountains where they held up a train and got away with $8,000. A posse caught them along the Powder River in Wyoming as the outlaws were eating supper around a campfire.

Curry escaped, rode south to Utah and was caught rustling cattle. A posse was quickly formed and after a six-mile running gunfight Curry was shot in the head. He managed to drag himself into a rock pile. The posse surrounded him and when he did not return fire they closed in. Curry had died quietly, slumped against a rock with his rifle in his lap.

In the grisly aftermath souvenir hunters stripped skin from Curry, tanned it, and turned the leather into wallets. Curry's father claimed what remained of the body and shipped it back to Nebraska for burial.

KING FISHER

King Fisher began his life of crime at the age of 15 when he stole a horse and rode out of Florence, Texas with the law chasing him. A year later he was captured and sentenced to 24 months in the state penitentiary.

After his release Fisher worked as a cowboy, breaking wild mustangs and, for sport, chasing down and killing Mexican bandits. He ruled with his gun, taking what he wanted from those who did not have the guts to face him and killing those who did. He acquired a reputation as a gaudy dresser, wearing fringed shirts, crimson sashes and bells on his spurs. He was accused of rustling several times but always managed to stay a step ahead of the law.

One time during a branding King became embroiled in an argument with several vaqueros. He dispatched his nearest opponent by hitting him over the head with the branding iron. When the second man went for his gun, King drew and shot him dead. Whirling he drilled two spectators who were sitting on the top rail of the corral.

In 1876 King married and eventually became the father of four daughters; but he never took to family life and over the years he was arrested for numerous murders. In each case he was found not guilty or the charges were dismissed.

After being acquitted of killing a Texas Ranger, through the dramatics of an expensive lawyer, King claimed his troubled life was behind him. He was sworn in as deputy sheriff of Uvalde County, pinned a star to his chest and rode with the law. Acting as deputy he shot and killed Tom Hannehan, one of two brothers suspected of robbing a stage.

The following year King was gunned down in an ambush in a San Antonio bar and buried in the Uvalde cemetery. Tom Hannehan's mother would visit the grave of King Fisher every anniversary of her son's death. She would set a bush on fire and "dance with devilish glee around the mound".

PAT GARRETT

The names of Pat Garrett and Billy The Kid will forever be entwined because it was Pat Garrett, the lawman, who gunned down the infamous outlaw.

Garrett was born in the deep south and after the death of his parents during the Civil War he headed west, spending several years punching cattle in the Texas Panhandle. It was during this time that he met William Bonney and, although the lad was ten years his junior, the two became good friends. In fact, as the two frequented the saloons and gambling establishments they became known as Big Casino and Little Casino, a reference to their size differences. Garrett stood 6'4" and Bonney was just a wisp of a kid.

By 1880 Garrett had been elected sheriff of Lincoln County, New Mexico and Bonney, better known as Billy the Kid, was the leader of a band of wild desperadoes. In fact, Garrett was elected, in part, because of his friendship with Billy the Kid. The leaders of the county figured Garrett would know where to find his friend and after a lengthy manhunt Garrett was successful. But the Kid killed two guards and escaped from jail. A year later, on a summer night in Fort Sumner, New Mexico, Garrett caught up with the Kid in a dark bedroom and gunned him down.

Some praised Garrett for the killing, others castigated him. He had to fight for the reward, threatening to sue before the state legislature would release it. When it came time for re-election Garrett's name was not allowed on the ballot. He turned his back on politics and, for a time, operated a cattle ranch near Las Cruces, New Mexico.

Garrett leased the ranch to a man who replaced the cattle with goats. They argued about this and Garrett was killed, supposedly in self-defense. Even though this was disputed the outcome remained the same - Pat Garrett, famous lawman and killer of Billy the Kid, was shot dead at the age of 57.

CHRISTMAS HOLD-UP

The James boys, Frank and Jesse, got away with robbing six banks over a four-year period without being identified. But on the seventh holdup, the Davies County Savings Bank at Gallatin, Missouri, they got tagged.

It was just before Christmas 1869. Frank held the horses while Jesse strolled inside and asked the teller to change a $10 bill. As the cashier complied, Jesse leaned across the counter and peered into his face, concluding, "I remember you. You killed a friend of mine in the war."

"No, no, no ... you got the wrong man. I was never in the war," stammered the cashier. Jesse shot him anyway, wrenched the bill from his hand and scooped $700 from the cash drawer.

Before Jesse reached the door Frank was exchanging shots with several men who had rushed to the scene. Frank handed Jesse his reins and wheeled his horse around to escape the deadly gunfire. Jesse grabbed hold of the saddle horn and started to swing up but the horse, panicked by the hail of bullets, reared. Jesse's foot slipped through the stirrup and the horse dragged him a ways before he could work himself free. The horse ran away and Jesse was left in the dusty street with shots ricocheting all around him.

Frank took a quick look over his shoulder, saw what had happened and turned back. Jesse leaped up behind him and they rode double to the edge of town where they relieved a man of his horse and completed their escape.

The posse did manage to capture the runaway horse and it was soon identified as belonging to Jesse James. The James boys were branded outlaws and a $3,000 reward was placed on their heads.

FAIR FIGHT

"Long as we're on the subject of gunfights I saw this with my own two eyes," the old man told the group of buckaroos seated around the campfire. He took a sip of black coffee from his tin cup and related the following story:

"This would've been 'long 'bout 18 and 84, maybe '85. We had just finished drivin' 2,000 head of longhorn steers to market. We were in a saloon an' havin' ourselves a good time of it, drinkin' whiskey an' the like.

"Anyways, one of the men in our outfit, Jim was his name, just a little fellar, soakin' wet he'd go maybe a hundred an' thirty pounds, not any more'n that, but he was tough as a railroad spike an' rumor had it Jim was a gunfighter of some renown.

"He packed a pair of Peacemakers, .45 caliber, with fancy scroll work on the cylinder and barrel and mother-of-pearl grips into which was carved an eagle with a snake in its mouth. I know for a fact Jim was lightning fast on the draw an' deadly as sin 'cause I seen him one time, just fer kicks, toss a tin can in the air and empty both guns into it 'fore it hit the ground.

"Gettin' back to that night in the saloon - I don't rightly know what caused it, but Jim gets in a beef with this big fellar, head an' hide go 250 pounds. They square off. But somebody must've called somethin' to the big fellar 'bout Jim bein' a professional, 'cause he starts to lose his nerve, protests to the saloonkeep, 'Wait a minute. He's a little bitty target. I'm way bigger. This ain't a fair fight.'

"Jim turns to the saloonkeep an' drawls, 'Why don't ya take a piece of chalk an' make an outline my size on this fellar. Any of my slugs outside the line don't count.'

"An' that was all it took. The big man backed down."

HELLS CANYON FEUD

Two ranchers, Fred Myers and C.J. Hall, ran cattle in Hells Canyon and competed for rangeland. Several small incidents between the two outfits festered into a feud that finally exploded into gunfire.

Myers had a place on the upper end of Big Bar with an alfalfa field ready to cut for hay. Two of Hall's men, Abbie Brownlee and Wallace Garrett, were bringing a herd of cattle past Big Bar and rather than go around, they opened the gate and drove the cattle through the alfalfa.

Myers was at his cabin when he heard the sounds of cattle on the move. On the way out the door he grabbed his rifle and shot and killed Brownlee. The second shot hit Garrett in the hand and the third knocked down his horse. Garrett took off on foot and hid in a cave until dark.

Word of the killing spread and a group of men sympathetic to Myers gathered at his ranch. They offered to accompany him to Grangeville, Idaho, where he had the best chance of receiving a fair trial. It was a two-day trip and that evening, in the town of Whitebird, Myers was placed in jail for his own protection.

During the night a lynch mob of Hall sympathizers broke down the jailhouse door and took Myers. When Sheriff Smallwood arrived from Grangeville to claim the prisoner he found him hanging in a tree. As he was cutting down the body a group of riders assembled.

The sheriff admonished them with, "You're nothin' but a pack of murderers." He looked hard and mean at each rider and finally stopped at one man, a prominent rancher - the only man who did not have a lariat tied to his saddle.

The sheriff addressed the rancher, "You're the ring leader. Only thing, I can't prove it." He tossed the hangman's rope to the rancher and without saying another word departed with the body of Fred Myers.

THUNDERING RIDE

The fall of 1871 two professional hunters, Jim Caspion and Sam Tillman, were traveling horseback across the rolling plains of western Kansas looking for buffalo to kill. They were riding apart, but within sight of each other.

"I reached the top of a long ridge," related Caspion, "looked over the edge and saw below a great herd of buffalo grazing peacefully. I turned in the saddle to signal my partner. That was when I observed that Tillman was engaged in a run for his life, attempting to outrace a party of about 50 Cheyenne warriors. I was powerless to lend a hand and was forced to be an observer as they ran him down, killed and scalped him. For several minutes they paraded around displaying the coup, which they borne aloft on a lance. Then suddenly they leaped on their horses and started for me.

"I was a mile away. My only route of escape was over the ridge and that was the way I went, spurring my horse straight toward the buffalo herd.

"They stampeded around me and I was swallowed up in a seething mass of boiling, choking, white dust. Buffalo were jostling my horse as we galloped blindly across the uneven ground. Their hooves, striking the sun-baked ground, gave off a noise that filled the air like rolling thunder.

"For 20 miles we rode that hard-charging buffalo wave and then all of a sudden the herd divided. My horse pulled back at the very precipice of a tall cliff and I watched, transfixed, by the spectacle before my eyes as animals leaped off into space. I listened to the dull thuds as they fell to the rocks below; those not killed outright bellowed in pain.

"My horse and I were swept along into the safe arms of a broad valley where I dropped to the ground and collapsed from a combination of exhaustion and fear."

CROSSING HICKOK

Philip Coe was a Texas gambler who crossed Marshal Wild Bill Hickok and paid for it with his life.

Coe operated the Bull's Head Saloon. Located on the outskirts of Abilene, Kansas, it was the first drinking and gambling establishment encountered by cowboys coming off the long cattle drives. On the evening of October 5, 1871 a group of about 50 Texas cowboys hit town. They were in a festive mood and Coe drank with them. Their activities were confined to the Bull's Head but soon the party spilled into the streets where cowboys grabbed passersby, carried them inside and made them buy drinks.

At one point Marshal Hickok showed up, bought the men a round and warned, "I know it's been a long, dusty trail. I'm not against you having a little fun but I don't want nobody gettin' hurt. Above all, I don't want no shootin'." That said, the marshal departed and continued his rounds.

During the drunken celebration that followed shots were fired and Hickok returned. He approached the merrymakers and demanded to know who had fired his weapon. Coe stepped forward. "I did. What are you going to do about it?"

Hickok's hand went for his gun but Coe got off a quick shot that drilled a hole through the marshal's coat. Then Hickok fired a big slug into Coe's belly. Just then deputy Mike Williams rushed around the corner and Hickok, fearing more trouble, whirled and fired twice. Both slugs hit Williams in the head, killing him instantly. With that horrible deed, Hickok called out, "The fun is over. I'm locking up town."

Coe was taken to his room. He lingered four long, agonizing days and then mercifully his maker called him home.

MASSACRE AND REVENGE

On the evening of October 7, 1855, in a Jacksonville, Oregon saloon, a large group of men gathered. They drank and talked about the bad blood between the miners and the Indians of the region. There was much boasting about deeds of bravery and some bragged about Indians they had killed.

Passions were running high when Major James Lupton, a member-elect of the Oregon territorial legislature, shouted above the din, "Let's organize a war party. I'll lead. We'll get ourselves a few scalps. Who's with me?"

It was popular proposal and after a few more drinks Major Lupton led a group of men out of town to an Indian camp along the Rogue River. A small band of Indians, a group who had always acted in a friendly manner toward the miners and settlers, were camped there near a landmark called Table Rock.

In the dark the white men surrounded the camp and as sunrise flushed the sky blood red, a volley was fired into the peaceful camp. Major Lupton gave the order to charge and more Indians were killed with revolvers, knives and clubs.

During the battle Major Lupton was struck with a poison arrow, a wound from which he later died. The vigilante killers returned to the settlement, proudly waving the scalps they had taken and expecting a heroes' reception. But it was learned that most of the Indians in the camp were old men, women and children and the men who had participated in the massacre were branded as cowards.

The senseless attack was followed by acts of revenge as Indians waylaid miners and freighters, burned homestead cabins and killed settlers. And, in turn, more Indians were killed. This frightful time became known as the Rogue River Indian War.

DEATH OF JESSE JAMES

In 1882 Bob Ford was a baby-faced 21-year-old living with his family in Ray County, Missouri. During an argument at his sister's house he killed a man, wrapped him in a horse blanket and buried the body in the woods.

When he was questioned about the killing he bragged to authorities that he was friends with Jesse James. Missouri Governor Thomas Crittendon spoke personally with the boy and promised that if he would kill the famous outlaw he would be given a full pardon and receive a $10,000 reward.

At the time Jesse James claimed he was retired and was living in St. Joseph under the assumed name of Mr. Howard. But the retirement was to be short-lived. Another robbery was being planned and Bob Ford and his older brother Charlie were supposed to be in on the crime.

On the morning of April 3, 1882 the brothers entered the James house. Jesse was standing on a chair straightening a picture on the wall. Bob recognized this moment as the opportunity he had been waiting for and fired a bullet into the back of Jesse James's skull.

Jesse's wife ran into the room. Bob, holding the smoking murder weapon in his hand, shrugged and said, "It went off accidently." He and Charlie dashed out the door to the telegraph office where Bob sent a message to the governor claiming the $10,000 reward.

Since Jesse James was a popular figure, the Ford brothers were regarded with widespread contempt. Charlie soon committed suicide while Bob became a member of P.T Barnum's freak show. He was jeered at nearly every stop and eventually left the tour. Later he operated a saloon in Las Vegas, New Mexico and then established a saloon in a tent in the Colorado boom town of Creede. It was here on the 8th of June, 1892 that Bob Ford met his violent end, gunned down by a shotgun slug that hit him in his throat.

OUTLAW ROOTS

Many of the Western outlaws had their roots in the Civil War. As victory in that bitter conflict swung toward the Union forces, Confederate troops broke away rather than surrender. These renegade bands continued fighting, harassing northern troops whenever they could as well as attacking unprotected frontier settlements and killing those who held allegiance to the Union.

One infamous raid occurred in August 1863 when 450 raiders led by William Quantrill swept into Lawrence, Kansas, a well-known Union settlement. Town was burned to the ground and 150 civilians were murdered.

Another notorious group was Anderson's Raiders, named after the leader, Bloody Bill Anderson. In 1864 the raiders, numbering 225, attacked Centralia, Missouri. They pillaged town and ambushed the train when it arrived. Twenty-five Union soldiers were gunned down, passengers were robbed and $3,000 was stolen from the express car.

The Civil War ended but there was no turning back for the renegade soldiers. They survived because they had the support of the residents living on the frontier. Many of them were former Confederate soldiers who had returned home and found their farms and families ravaged by the war. The outlaw gangs rode against the tight-fisted banks, the rich stagecoach lines and monopolistic railroad companies. They became heros to the legion of more peaceful men who admired the rebellious nature of the gunfighters.

Slowly local residents rebuilt their lives and resumed farming. Roads and rails tied remote settlements together and residents of these towns became civilized. Their opinions and sentiments changed. The wild element was no longer to be tolerated and the outlaw was pushed farther west, until finally, no place existed in society for the gunfighter.

Rick Steber's Tales of the Wild West Series is available in hardbound books ($14.95) and paperback books ($4.95) featuring illustrations by Don Gray, as well as in audio tapes ($7.95) narrated by Dallas McKennon. Current titles in the series include:

- ❑ *OREGON TRAIL* Vol. 1 *
- ❑ *PACIFIC COAST* Vol. 2 *
- ❑ *INDIANS* Vol. 3 *
- ❑ *COWBOYS* Vol. 4 *
- ❑ *WOMEN OF THE WEST* Vol. 5 *
- ❑ *CHILDREN'S STORIES* Vol. 6 *
- ❑ *LOGGERS* Vol. 7 *
- ❑ *MOUNTAIN MEN* Vol. 8 *
- ❑ *MINERS* Vol. 9 *
- ❑ *GRANDPA'S STORIES* Vol. 10
- ❑ *PIONEERS* Vol. 11
- ❑ *CAMPFIRE STORIES* Vol. 12
- ❑ *TALL TALES* Vol. 13
- ❑ *GUNFIGHTERS* Vol. 14

Available on Audio Tape

Other books written by Rick Steber include *ROUNDUP, OREGON TRAIL -- LAST OF THE PIONEERS, HEARTWOOD, NEW YORK TO NOME, WILD HORSE RIDER, WHERE ROLLS THE OREGON, TRACES*, and *RENDEZVOUS*.

If unavailable at retailers in your area write directly to the publisher. A catalog is free upon request.

Bonanza Publishing
Box 204
Prineville, Oregon 97754